DALE EARNHARDT JR.

DISCOVER THE LIFE OF A SPORTS STAR II

David and Patricia Armentrout

Rourke

Publishing LLC
Vero Beach, Florida 32964

www.rourkepublishing.com

PHOTO CREDITS:
Cover ©Doug Pensinger/Getty Images; Cover, Pages 5, 19 ©Rusty Jarrett; Title, pages 4, 7, 15 ©Jon Ferrey/Getty Images; Pages 6, 12 ©Robert Laberge/Getty Images; Page 10 ©Brian Cleary/Getty Images; Page 8 ©Peter Carvelli/Getty Images; Pages 17, 21 ©Donald Miralle/Getty Images; Page 18 ©Jamie Squire/Getty Images

Title page: *Dale Jr.'s pit crew works fast in order to get No. 8 back on track.*

Editor: Frank Sloan

Cover and interior design by Nicola Stratford

Library of Congress Cataloging-in-Publication Data

Armentrout, David, 1962-
 Dale Earnhardt, Jr. / David and Patricia Armentrout.
   p. cm. — (Discover the life of a sports star II)
 Includes bibliographical references (p.   ) and index.
 ISBN 1-59515-132-X (hardcover)
 1. Earnhardt, Dale, Jr.--Juvenile literature. 2. Automobile racing drivers--United States--Biography--Juvenile literature. I. Armentrout, Patricia, 1960- II. Title. III. Series: Armentrout, David, 1962- Discover the life of a sports star II.
 GV1032.E18A76 2004
 796.72'092--dc22

                                        2004007640

Printed in the USA

CG/CG

Table of Contents

Dale Jr. honors his grandfather Ralph Earnhardt by using his old racing number—8.

Dale Earnhardt Jr.

Dale Earnhardt Jr. races stock cars. He is one of the hottest new stars in stock car racing today. In fact, Dale Jr. was voted **NASCAR**'s most popular driver of 2003 by fans nationwide.

Born: October 10, 1974 in Concord, North Carolina
Competition: NASCAR's Nextel and Busch Series
Car: Chevrolet Monte Carlo
Number: 8
Record: Busch Series Champion 1998 and 1999; 2004 Daytona 500 Winner

It's a Family Thing

Interest in motor sports runs in the Earnhardt family. Dale Jr.'s grandfather, Ralph Earnhardt, raced cars from the 1950s to the 1970s. Dale Jr.'s father was racing legend Dale Earnhardt.

Dale and Teresa Earnhardt formed Dale Earnhardt, Inc. (DEI) in 1980. The company is involved in many aspects of motorsports. DEI designs and builds race cars and hires drivers like Dale Jr. for the DEI team.

Dale Jr. leads Kevin Harvick #29 at the 2003 Subway 500.

Dale Sr. and his wife Teresa pose with Dale Jr. at the end of the 1999 Bush series.

Junior prepares to race in New Hampshire.

Pro Racing Begins

Dale Jr. began his **professional** racing career at the age of 17. He raced in the Street Stock division at Concord Motorsport Park in North Carolina.

At age 19, Dale Jr. began racing in NASCAR's Late Model circuit. He performed well and decided to try his luck in the Busch **series**. The Busch series is one level below NASCAR's top series—the Nextel Cup (formerly the Winston Cup).

Dale Jr. leads Matt Kenseth during his last AC Delco 1999 Busch race.

The Busch Series

Dale Jr. entered his first Busch event in 1996 and a handful of races in 1997. In 1998, he took his first checkered flag (win) in April at the Coca-Cola 300. He finished the year winning the Busch **championship**.

In September, Dale Jr. was offered a contract worth $80 million with Anheuser-Busch. Dale signed on to drive the Budweiser car in the Winston cup through the 2004 season. Not bad for a driver who had not even raced in the elite level yet!

In action at the Las Vegas Speedway

The Winston Cup

Dale Jr. won the Busch championship again in 1999 and raced in the Winston Cup for the first time.

In 2000, Dale's first full year in the Winston Cup, he won two races and became the first **rookie** to win "The Winston," NASCAR's all-star race. Dale Jr. learned a lot in 2000 and looked forward to the next season.

NASCAR's Great Loss

Fans thought Dale Jr. had a good chance of winning the 2001 opening race—the Daytona 500.

The race was exciting until its tragic ending. Michael Waltrip and Dale Jr. crossed the finish line first and second. Their boss and teammate, Dale Sr., didn't finish the race. Dale Earnhardt hit the wall at around 200 miles (332 km) an hour. Doctors say Dale Earnhardt died instantly. Michael Waltrip and Dale Jr.'s excitement quickly turned to grief.

NASCAR's racing legend Dale Earnhardt

Back in Daytona

Dale Jr. continued to race, hoping it would help him cope with his father's death. However, racing did not seem to help, and he raced poorly.

Things changed July 7, 2001, at the Pepsi 400 in Daytona. Dale Jr. worried about racing on the track that had taken his father's life, but he drove well. In fact, he won the race. Fans screamed with delight as the other drivers surrounded Dale Jr. in Victory Lane. Junior announced to the crowd that he was dedicating his win to his father.

Celebrating with friends after winning the Pepsi 400 in Daytona

Dale Jr. talks with his crew before a practice run. He later won at Talladega Superspeedway in Alabama.

More Winston Wins

Dale Jr. began the 2002 season a new man. He was focused on driving and the family business. He had two victories and finished 11 times in the top five.

Dale Jr. had two Winston Cup wins in 2003 as well, and finished in the top five 13 times. He ended the season in third place in the point standings.

Dale Jr. talks with DEI teammate Michael Waltrip during a Winston Cup qualifying event.

First Daytona Win

Dale Jr. Opened the 2004 season with a win at the Daytona 500! He hopes to continue speeding along on that same track of success by making it a championship year. Besides racing in the next Nextel Cup series, Dale Jr. will also be involved in the Busch series as a car owner. Dale Jr. and Teresa Earnhardt are co-owners of Chance 2 Motorsports. They hired Martin Truex Jr. to race the full 2004 Busch series. Dale Jr. loves the Busch level and plans to compete in a couple of Busch races himself.

Dale Jr. rounds the bend traveling close to 200 miles (321 km) an hour at Bristol Motor Speedway in Tennessee.

Dates to Remember

1996   Races in first Busch event

1998   Wins the Busch championship

1999   Wins the Busch championship

2000   Wins Winston Cup rookie of the year
        and NASCAR's all-star race

2001   Father Dale Earnhardt dies February 18
        at the Daytona 500

2002   Wins two Winston Cup races and finishes
        11 in the top 5

2003   Wins two Winston Cup races and finishes
        13 in the top 5

2004   Wins the Daytona 500

Glossary

championship (CHAM pee uhn ship) — each driver is awarded points in a race, with winners earning the most. Drivers with the most points at the end of a season win the championship

NASCAR — National Association for Stock Car Auto Racing: the governing body for the Nextel Cup, Craftsman Truck, and Busch series, among others

professional (pruh FESH uh nuhl) — someone paid to participate

rookie (ROOK ee) — a first-year driver

series (SIHR eez) — a group of races that make up one season

Index

Further Reading

Stewart, Mark. *Dale Earnhardt, Jr.: Driven by Destiny.* Millbrook Press, 2003.

Poole, David. *Dale Earnhardt Jr.: Junior Achievement: The Dale Earnhardt Jr. Story.* Triumph Books, 2003.

White, Ben. *Nascar Racers: Today's Top Drivers.* Motorbooks International, 2003.

Websites To Visit

www.nascar.com

www.dalejr.com

www.daleearnhardtinc.com

About The Authors

David and Patricia Armentrout have written many nonfiction books for young readers. They have had several books published for primary school reading. The Armentrouts live in Cincinnati, Ohio, with their two children.